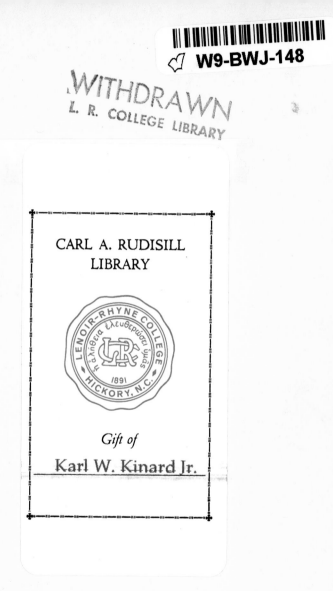

the
new song

leland b. sateren

a guide to modern music
for use in the church choir

AUGSBURG PUBLISHING HOUSE

minneapolis 15, minnesota

THE NEW SONG
© 1958 Augsburg Publishing House
Library of Congress Catalog Card No. 58-6616

Manufactured in the United States of America

Foreword

At the beginning of this century the music world was noisy with heated arguments and discussions over the changing musical language that was then being demonstrated in the work of such composers as Stravinsky, Bartok, Berg, and Schoenberg. The disputes soon ceased, however, when it became evident that the new language was not gibberish but, in fact, an expressive means of great and wonderful potential.

For a quarter of a century or more the new musical language, or "modern" music, has been the only language used by our greatest composers. The world of secular music has long since accepted this fact, at the same time retaining its rights of critical evaluation. Not all music written in the new idiom is of high quality, any more than music written in previous centuries. It is certain, however, that any music written today that does not make use of the new language forfeits its right to be judged at all. It is simply disregarded as an anachronistic curiosity.

This poses a real problem to church musicians which we cannot afford to ignore any longer. By restricting our service music lists to compositions of earlier centuries and to unimaginative and derivative contemporary works we are widening the distressing gap between the world of art music and the church which began to form almost two hundred years ago and which we must some day close if the music of the Church is ever to be restored to its former position of greatness. During these two hundred years the secular world has attracted and held the interests of most of the great composers because the Church has in large part withdrawn the support and encouragement that it accorded them formerly. The longer we persist in our neglect the more difficult it will be to repair the damage already done.

It is not easy to find an immediate or simple solution to a problem whose complexities involve factors outside the Church as well as within. This fact must not discourage us, however, for it is imperative that we do something about it. Professor Sateren faces the problem realistically and offers wise and helpful counsel on how it may be approached. His is the advice of a practising and understanding church musician, not that of a cultist, and his suggestions are presented with full appreciation of those many local problems with which all of us who work in church music must contend. His request is modest but nonetheless urgent: Take note of the "new song," heed its special meaning for our own time, and above all let it be heard.

Professor Sateren is not alone in making this plea. Many church musicians of all denominations throughout the country share his concern and support him wholeheartedly. They are using the new song and know well its power for expressing through music the vital message of the Church today. Let us keep the good that is old, but let us not neglect the good that is new, lest there some day be no good that is old.

LUTHER NOSS

School of Music
Yale University
December 8, 1957

Contents

Illustrations

Acknowledgments

For permission to quote from their publications, I am indebted to the following:

Augsburg Publishing House (Figures 3, 4, 10, 12, 15 and 16)
Summy-Birchard Publishing Company, Evanston, Illinois, (Figure 14)
Concordia Publishing House (Figure 13)
H. T. FitzSimons Company (Figures 2 and 5)
H. W. Gray Company (Figure 17)
Neil A. Kjos Music Company (Figures 6 and 19)
Mercury Music Corporation (Figure 18)
Oxford University Press (Figure 11)
Southern Music Company (Figure 1)

Gratitude is also due:

. . . Dr. Luther D. Noss, distinguished Chairman of the Department of Music, Yale University, for his kindness in writing the Foreword.

. . . Dr. James Aliferis, composer, conductor and teacher, Department of Music, University of Minnesota, for valuable suggestions.

. . . the members of the Senior Choir, Messiah Lutheran Church, Minneapolis, Minnesota. They have been a fruitful, stimulating proving-ground for many modern anthems. Together with their organist, Mrs. Bette Boyer Holmes, they have been among the forces contributing to the formulation of this guide.

. . . Miss Ruth Olson, of the Music Department of the Augsburg Publishing House, for her interest in "the new song" as a vital, significant means of worship, not to say her interest in the Ministry of Music in all its phases and in its finest expressions.

L. B. S.

Introduction

The purpose of this manual is twofold: (1) to state the more easily recognizable characteristics of "modern" music; and (2) to encourage the use of this musical language—the "new song"—in the Church.

It is aimed at the director of the parish choir, with a view to its use as a guide in the orientation (of the director, his choir, and the congregation), selection and performance of progressive music. While designed primarily for him, and restricted in its scope to sacred choral music, a good deal of the discussion would apply to modern music as a whole, and, therefore, may be found useful in such classroom courses as Conducting, Instrumental-Choral Materials, Literature, Interpretation and Analysis, etc.

Essentially, this is a primer. It is not an "apology" for the music of every modern composer. The knowledgeable musician will have to go elsewhere for a comprehensive treatment of the subject. The language is not highly technical, but assumes a rather limited musical training and/or an unfamiliarity with the techniques and devices, the stuff of modern music.

The illustrations are representative of a middle path: they stop considerably short of atonality, but are in advance of "conventional" church choir music. All of them are excerpts from pieces which have been sung by parish choirs, and cannot, therefore, be dismissed by the sceptical director as "impossible in the 'practical' situation of the church choir." Not all of the anthems can be performed by a small group—since divided parts occasionally are required, but the quotations from them can nevertheless serve as guides to the language.

The chief problem for the director who sets out to minister through the "new song" is the one of learning to "hear" modern music—that is, of accustoming himself to its sounds and, then, of responding to them, of letting the auditory stimulus (the music as it is sung by the choir, or as it is played by the organist) arouse and intensify his religious emotion. The experience of being communicated to by the "new song" will prove its value many times over. Once the hurdles of hearing and unfamiliarity are behind, modern music speaks with a relevancy that cannot be resisted, in a language that ministers uniquely to the soul of the worshipper.

LELAND B. SATEREN

THE NEW SONG

Sing unto him a new song. —Psalm 33:3

" '*Modern*' music for my church choir? Do you mean the kind of music that I think I don't like, that I can't direct, that my choir can't sing, and that the congregation doesn't like?"

"After all, I'm just an average director; maybe not even average, because my training is limited."

"And then there's my choir—some of my basses have a hard time singing up and down a scale, let alone singing some of those tough intervals."

"As for the congregation, I know it doesn't like modern music—the kind I think you mean. They want only what they've been getting. Why bother them with something they didn't ask for?"

"Still, since you raised the question, I'll go along and expose my ignorance by asking a few questions. I may be naive, but:

"Is there 'modern' music for the *parish* choir? If there is, what about using it? Is there a 'case' for it? What is it like? How does it differ from the 'traditional' music we've been using?"

"Assuming for a minute that I might want to try some

1

of it, how can I prepare myself—as a director? How about preparing the choir? And the congregation?"

"Between the two of us, I really don't know much about this kind of music. The blunt fact is that I wouldn't know my way around in it at all. Consequently, I feel safer if I stick with what we've been doing. No director wants to parade his weaknesses."

*　　*　　*

These sentiments and questions aren't imaginary. They are not the exclusive property of only a few directors. Probably even the most successful and progressive will tell you that somewhere and sometime along the way they felt pretty much as you do, and they asked the same questions. Many of them served in positions similar to the one you are in right now.

Since frankness begets frankness, it might give you some comfort to know that most church choir directors would respond to your reactions with a fairly fervent, "Me, too!" In short, you aren't alone; your company is legion.

It would be absurd, for example, to presume that all parish choir directors are attracted to, like, and perform modern music. A realistic appraisal would find a large percentage of them shying away from it for the reasons you implied or stated: (a) they're pretty sure they don't like it, (b) it strikes them as beyond the capabilities of themselves and their choirs, and (c) they are "afraid of what the congregations will think."

All the same, the director who views his ministry as a continuing challenge, and who has a notion that there *night* be something for himself and his people in this type of music ought to be encouraged. His present sentiments deserve consideration. His questions are fair and, if answers are possible, they should be given.

Before proceeding, let's stop long enough for a few observations.

Introductory Remarks

The ways in which we express ideas change. The language we use in conversation is not the language, say, of Chaucer. The spelling is different, the pronunciation is different, and the sentence construction is different.

If we examine Thomas Jefferson's script on the Declaration of Independence, we know that his style of writing isn't ours.

We know that certain architectural lines have conveyed the idea of a church; no one has had to tell us, "This is a church." But we know that churches built at the beginning of this century differ considerably from those being built nowadays: lines and materials are used in new ways, and we call the result "modern church architecture."

Means and methods of worshipping change, too, and we've undoubtedly seen such changes take place. As in life generally, there is also in the Church a continual sifting; what was once effective is discarded as its usefulness ceases. New means and fresh methods evolve. When this process isn't going on, we say we've "gone stale."

Since we are concerned with church music, it is worth mentioning that this art has been most creative and most adventurous when the religious life of the composer has

been at high tide. Music has been a powerful expressio
of this life.

An idea which really gets hold of us virtually force
us to say—as best we can—what the idea means. If th
idea overwhelms us or, more specifically now, if we hav
been gripped by the message of Christianity, we aren
nearly so apt to ask, "How did Father (or Dave, Johann
Mary or Kirsten) say what this meant to him?" as, "How
can *we* say what it means?"

Essentially, the answer to the latter question—given i
terms of melody, harmony and rhythm—has been the wor
of the composer of music for the Church. And when h
imagination has been flooded with a religious truth, h
has not only tried to express his grasp of the idea, bu
has reached out for new ways of saying it. Where ther
is real vitality, each generation is inspired to say *in it
language* what the Faith means.

This is certainly a part of what the Psalmist meant whe
he wrote about "a new song." He probably wasn't sug
gesting that we shouldn't sing "an old song"—on the con
trary, he would likely have agreed that there are man
old songs worthy of being sung. But singling out th
new song seems to recognize, by implication, that (a) th
old song is not enough in the wake of a profound religiou
experience, and (b) the vitality arising from this expe
rience searches out new ways of expression.

If all this seems far-fetched, all we need to do for il
lustration is to look to the great religious music of Pales
trina, Schütz and Bach. Time has given us a chance t
assess their works in relation to their lives, and we know
they were not simply tunesmiths or lackeys turning ou

tunes for the fun of it. They had religious sentiments that could be expressed in no other way than through the genius of their art: and either they fashioned "new songs" or so apotheosized the old that it seemed to their contemporaries the utterance of a later day.

What about today? Are composers singing "a new song"? Are they reaching out for new ways of expressing religious ideas? Modern music is heard in concert halls, you say; but in our churches? And if it is not heard in our churches, does this mean that modern sacred music is not being composed?

It is being written—in surprisingly large quantities. Therefore, you and directors like yourself—interested, but not at all sure when it comes to finding and working with this "new song"—may find it helpful to discuss some of its characteristics, several examples, and a few suggestions respecting its introduction to your choir and congregation —since it is fair to assume that, for favorable response, they are entitled to some of the preparation you believe you require.

Characteristics of "Modern" Music

To begin with, it should be clear that "modern" and "contemporary" are not necessarily synonymous terms. A choir anthem may be both, but it may also be a contemporary piece which is in no sense "modern." In fact, most of the music being written for church choirs today is not modern, although it is contemporary.

What is meant by "modern music for the church choir"? Confining ourselves to the music only (no reference to text), and to a general statement, it may be said that the idiom of modern music (its melody, harmony and rhythm) is progressive.

(1) In its surrounding harmony, melody often seems to lack what is thought of as "lyric" quality;

(2) Its harmony goes beyond, or is an advance of, conventional love-song and hymnbook harmony—so-called "traditional" harmony; or it utilizes the old Modes;

(3) Its rhythm is often quite free—deferring to the natural stresses of the words being sung; in the musical development, the rhythm may exploit, say, syncopation and cross-accents for what they may do in evoking the sense of a given text.

To these generalizations dealing largely with objective facts we should add one on the subjective side:

(4) The serious composer of modern music for the church choir tries to come to grips with the essential meaning and spirit of the text he is setting—beyond, that is, using a diminished-seventh chord to express fear or anguish.

Detail and Illustrations

A. MELODY

Irrespective of their merits, the opening section of Brahms' *How Lovely Is Thy Dwelling Place*, Shelley's *The King of Love My Shepherd Is*, and *Beautiful Savior*, in F. Melius Christiansen's well-known arrangement, have been widely used among church choirs. There is no question that the lyric character of their melodies has contributed to their popularity. One may or may not care for every harmony used, for the rhythms employed in this section

r that, for the use of humming, for the high tenor part
ere or the difficult bass interval there, etc. But the lyric
uality of their tunes cannot be denied: the melodies
eem to sing themselves. If they fail, it is only because
he choir or the director (or both) "got in the way."

This quality of lyricism seems absent from many of the
unes of modern composers. Undoubtedly, *unfamiliarity*
1akes some of them sound less lyric than they are; but
he composer will insist his melody is altogether songful.
-More often than not, the composer is right, and if we
ive his tunes a chance, we will find them lyric, indeed.

Chosen at random, here are melodies from three mod-
rn anthems:

igure 1   (Lockwood: *Let Nothing Disturb Thee*)

Let noth-ing __ dis-turb __ thee, Let noth-ing af - fright __ thee;

All __ things are pass - ing;   God nev-er, nev-er chang - eth;

>pyright 1955 Southern Music Co., San Antonio, Texas

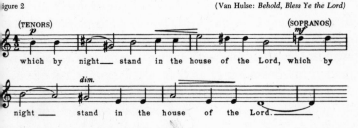

igure 2   (Van Hulse: *Behold, Bless Ye the Lord*)

(TENORS)   (SOPRANOS)

which by   night __ stand   in the house of the Lord, which by

night __   stand   in   the   house   of   the   Lord. __

Figure 3

(P. Christiansen: *Chorale from "Invocation and Chorale"*)

Copyright 1956 Augsburg Publishing House, Minneapolis, Minnesota

If you sing these tunes until they are memorized, you will find their singing quality reasonably compelling. They are predominantly scalewise, with occasional simple intervals (as opposed to awkward leaps) whose tonal reference is diatonic, their rhythms are uncomplicated, and so on.

Had you first heard them *in the context of their more or less dissonant harmony,* however, your judgment of their lyric character might have been quite different.

It may generally be said that the melodies of composers of modern choral music are as singable, as lyric as any of "the good old songs." On occasion they are angular (rather than scalewise) and of considerable intervallic freedom, but any number of the vocal lines of Bach and Brahms will show the same thing.

The difference between the old and the modern is not in the essential lyric quality of the melodies, but in the *har-*

monic context, in the harmonies which surround them. In the case of the modern composer, this context tends to be *dissonant;* in the others, it is basically *consonant.*

B. HARMONY

The harmonic resources available to the composer of today have vastly increased music's expressive possibilities, permitting music to delineate almost every shade in the spectrum of ideas and the feeling-states they evoke.

As with melody, so also in harmony have tradition and association played powerful roles in music for the church choir. They have, in fact, produced the anthem stereotype alluded to earlier.

The prevailing and usually immediately acceptable harmonic idiom is overwhelmingly Romantic in character; and in its baser forms in church music it is sometimes spoken of as "Victorian."

Romantic harmony is marked by its warmth, often by its richness—its sometimes opulent, lush color, frequently by its predictability (that is, one can anticipate each successive harmony, as well as the treatment that will be given to a text), and, at its worst, by cliches which are referred to charitably as "sentimental."

The criterion upon which a good deal of Romantic harmony is based is, "Is this 'nice'; will it give pleasure to the listener?"

In contrast, the composer of modern music for the church choir is not primarily concerned with "nice" harmony, or with the "pleasure" his harmony will give the listener. His approach to harmonic devices as they exist today tends to be functional and utilitarian. He shuns unnecessary adornments—because he believes they divert the attention—and asks only one question: *Does this harmony, better than any other, evoke what seems to be the essential spirit of this text?*

What one hears in his anthem then, judged by Romantic harmony, may be spare, bald, dry, objective, even cold. And when the text demands, he will use chords whose tensions are severe and sometimes almost brutal.

The response may be one of music that is not "liked," but this is not the final test in the mind of the composer, since he doesn't regard pleasurable listening or the response of being liked as the end-all of effective choir music. The crucial matter for him is whether or not he has set forth the spirit of the text. If his listener can assure him he has at least done this, the composer is content.

It may be said at this point that, whatever its merits, music of this type commands attention: We cannot doze through it or, if awake, reject it. The music forces us to listen, to attend.

The following anthem quotations demonstrate how each composer has used various harmonic tensions to convey his understanding of the text:

Figure 4

(Sateren: *The Word Rejected*)

Figure 5   (Van Hulse: *Behold, Bless Ye the Lord*)

Figure 6

(P. Christiansen: *As a Flower of the Field*)

Among the elements contributing to the spare, bald sounds of modern music is the open or "empty" chord: the chord without its "character note." (See figure 5, voice parts, first beat, measure 7.) When the device is used extensively in a piece, the composer is utilizing one of the earliest known forms of harmony, called "organum." Figure 12 provides an example of this type of harmonization.

The paradox of the very old (organum) becoming the very new is also found in the rediscovery of the beauties of the modes, those ancient scales upon which the music of the early Church was based. Their association, in mod-

ern ears, is largely "church;" and this associative value
is a significant factor for any composer of church music.

For our purposes here we cite the eight so-called
Church Modes, transposed so they can be played on the
white keys of the piano:

Figure 7   * The four *Principal* modes. The remaining four are *Secondary*.

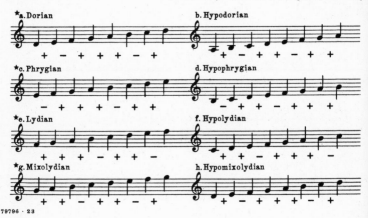

79796 · 23

The modes impart a minor cast to the music, but for
most people their distinctive flavor derives from the ab-
sence of the raised seventh (si) of the harmonic minor
scale. Among modal hymntunes, perhaps the best-known
is *O Sacred Head, Now Wounded,* the first phrase of
which is:

Figure 8   (Hassler: *O Sacred Head, Now Wounded*)

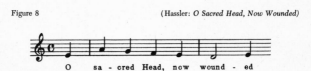

O   sa - cred Head, now wound - ed

If you reduce the tune to the scale upon which it is based, and compare it with the modes in Figure 7, you find that it matches the Phrygian.

You may suppose that you really can't tell the difference between a modal melody and one in minor, but the same phrase written in the nearest harmonic minor scale sounds quite different:

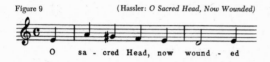

Figure 9   (Hassler: *O Sacred Head, Now Wounded*)

O   sa - cred Head, now   wound - ed

Here are excerpts from two modal anthems:

Figure 10   (Lovelace: *Only-Begotten, Word of God Eternal*)

Male Voices

Broadly

On - ly be - got - ten, Word of God e - ter - nal,

Piano or Organ

Manual

Lord of cre - a - tion, mer - ci - ful and might - y, Hear now Thy ser - vants,

when their joy-ful voic-es Rise ____ to Thy pres-ence.

Figure 11 (Oldroyd: *Prayer to Jesus*)

SOPRANO
ALTO

Jhe-su, since Thou must do ____ Thy

TENOR
BASS

will, And nae-thing is ____ that Thee ____ may

let, With— Thy grace —— my heart —— ful - fil,— My

love— and my lik - ing in Thee —— is set.—

This utilization in modern harmony of several of the techniques of very early music is also reflected in contemporary uses of polyphony—voice imitations such as we find, for example, in Handel's *Hallelujah Chorus* at the sections beginning, "For the Lord God Omnipotent reigneth," and, "And he shall reign forever and ever." (The term "polyphony" does not necessarily imply strict, verbatim imitation so much as it embodies the idea of each voice singing an independent, moving part—a melody). The result, when used by moderns, is not always strikingly different from the polyphony of early church composers. In others, though the technique is fairly obvious, the *sound* is clearly of another day, as the following shows:

Figure 12

(Sateren: *Thou Alone Art God*)

Finally, a composer may write in the modern idiom not because he has chosen to use progressive harmony, complex rhythmic patterns, etc., but because, as a "child of this day," it is his musical language. That is, beyond using the stuff of modern harmony to evoke more or less obvious sentiments, he will use it even in passages where the evocation of a specific sentiment is not necessary. He uses it because it is his means of expressing himself musically; it is for him as honest and natural a way of speaking in music as it is for the Southerner to talk with his delightful drawl.

C. RHYTHM

The music of the early Church was rhythmically free. Rhythms were determined by the natural accents of the words being sung, tempered only by such emotional stresses as their meanings aroused. Measured music, with its bar-lines and ordered, regular stresses, is a relatively recent invention.

Plainsong (chant) and the chorales of the early Lutheran Church (the chorales in their original, so-called "rhythmic" forms) are examples of music that is rhythmically free.

In addition to flowing with matchless grace, this type of music possesses a vitality that is difficult to equal in measured music. The rugged vigor of the rhythmic form of *A Mighty Fortress Is Our God,* for instance, is almost completely lost in the equal-note, barred version found in most hymnals.

As a general rule, composers writing rhythmically free music today use bar-lines, partly to facilitate reading, but primarily to indicate points of stress. No time signature is given because the metrical organization may differ from measure to measure, as in the following excerpt where the from-measure-to-measure organization is 2-4, 2-4, 3-8, 3-4, 2-4, 3-4, 5-8, 2-4, 4-4 and 4-4:

Figure 13   (Sateren: *To Such Belongeth the Kingdom*)

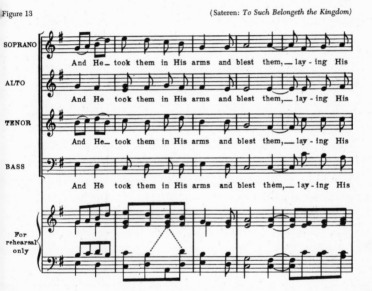

Music continues on next page

The composer of *Treasures in Heaven* (Fig. 14) gives a footnote stating, "As the rhythm is free, no time signature is given. Accents should be governed entirely by the natural accents of the words, not by the bar-lines."

(See also Figure 11 for an excellent example of this structural technique.)

Figure 14   (Clokey: *Treasures in Heaven*)

lay up for your-selves treas - ures in heav'n, for where your

lay up for your-selves treas - ures in heav'n, for where your

treas-ure is, there will your heart_____ be al - so.

treas-ure is, there will your heart_____ be al - so.

Figure 15   (Manz: *On My Heart Imprint Thine Image*)

Occasionally the modern composer employs a mixed plainsong-measured style, as in the preceding excerpt from *On My Heart Imprint Thine Image.*

Although preserving the form of measured music throughout, the sense of a regular pattern of accents in the following has been largely destroyed, and the effect is quite like plainsong:

Figure 16   (P. Christiansen: *The Annunciation*)

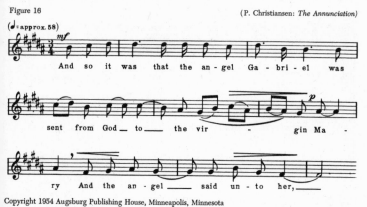

Rhythmic freedom and gentle harmonies impart a feeling of great serenity to these measures, in which, incidentally the composer has indicated each metre change:

Figure 17   (Jennings: *When to the Temple Mary Went*)

And when we must from earth de-part-ure take,

And when we must from earth de-part-ure take,

And when we must from earth de-part-ure take,

And when we must from earth de-part-ure take,

May gent - ly fall a - sleep,

May gent - ly fall a - sleep,

May gent - ly fall a - sleep,

May gent - ly fall a - sleep,

More often than not, composers of modern music for
the church choir use the forms of measured music, but
within that framework add vitality and intensity by means
of syncopation, cross-accents, etc. These examples illus-
trate the technique:

Figure 18

(Moe: *Hosanna to the Son of David*)

THE NEW SONG

Figure 19

(P. Christiansen: *Sing Unto the Lord*)

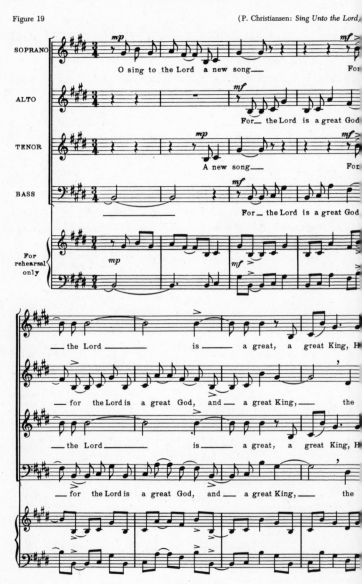

Directing Free Rhythm Music

Long before this point you may have given up with, "I might as well forget it because I have all I can manage just directing straight time, let alone all these changes."

The solution really is not difficult—if you are willing to *practice*. And why shouldn't you? Your choir and the congregation have a right to expect this of you.

"Practice what?"

Practice directing!

"How?"

Here is a directing routine that many have found beneficial; try it:

Using a moderate tempo and the quarter-note as the pulse unit (up to the point of the 8th-note signatures, where the 8th-note becomes the unit for beating), direct —without pause as you go from metre to metre—4 measures each of the signatures as indicated:

2-4 (The same pattern is used for 2-8 and 2-2):

3-4 (The same pattern is
        used for 3-8 and 3-2):

3-2 (Continue beating
        for the quarter-note):

4-4 (The same pattern is
        used for 4-8 and 4-2):

5-4 (Accent 1 and 3: 1-2-3-4-5):

5-4 (Accent 1 and 4: 1-2-3-4-5):

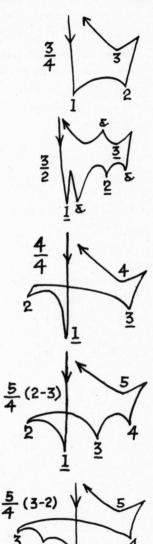

6-4 (The same pattern
    is used for 6-8):

9-8 (The same pattern
    is used for 9-4):

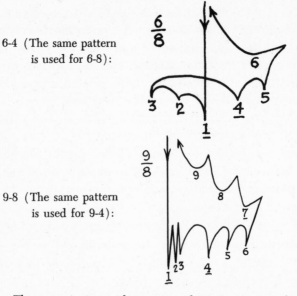

Then, continuing without pause, beat 1 measure of
12-8 (The same pattern is used for 12-4):

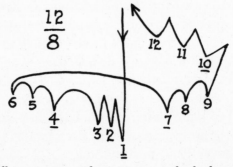

Still continuing without pause, go back through all
metres, beating one measure of each, thus:
9-8, 6-4, 5-4, (1-2-3-4-5), 5-4 (1-2-3-4-5), 4-4, 3-2 (beating for the quarter-note as before), 3-4 and 2-4 (holding
the last beat).

It is a good idea, at least to begin with, to count aloud as you direct the routine. But the important thing is that you direct it—don't sit down and imagine it. You should go through it until the patterns and the shifts from metre to metre become automatic, until you no longer have to think consciously of where the next beat goes.

When you have arrived at this point (it won't take you long if you practice), begin mixing the metres. For example: 6-8, 3-2, 5-4 (1-2-3-4-5), 9-8, 2-4, etc. You will find that before long you can move from metre to metre without the slightest difficulty. If you are unable to, the fault is yours: You haven't practiced enough!

In such rhythmically free anthems as carry no time signatures, you may want to write in the metre whenever it changes. This would be a perfectly logical part of your preparation of the piece.

You may at first feel a little awkward as you direct it, but never mind, you will soon direct it gracefully and without conscious effort; and then you can devote yourself to interpretation, quality, ensemble, and so on.

Occasionally you may find a piece in which the metrical structures of the various parts do not coincide. (For a modern example, see Lockwood's *Psalm 134.* The music of the early polyphonic masters—Palestrina, des Pres, Gibbons, et al.—is filled with these "dislocations." In most present-day editions, however, they have been largely ignored in favor of conventional mensuration.)

In directing music of this type two options are open: (1) you may beat for the part you regard as the more important, or (2) you may "set the pace" with a beat in which the feeling is simply 1-1-1-1-1, etc.: a more or less elliptical pattern, in clockwise direction and on a vertical plane.

The use of the various devices discussed under A, B and C is no idle, capricious effect. No sincere, serious composer displays technique for its own sake. He does not *try* to be complex, queer, strange, difficult, significant, a pioneer, or what have you.

You should not, therefore, impatiently dismiss his piece. On the contrary, look to *see why* the composer has elected to do as he did. After a careful study of the relationship between text and musical substance, you may not only be impressed with the music as music, but come away with such a grasp of the text as you have not had heretofore—meanings you had not imagined until the music suggested them to you.

The New Song and the Director

The key to the success of any choir is the director. It follows that he is also the key to the successful introduction and use of modern music in his choir.

In addition to acquainting yourself with the characteristics of the new song, what more can you do by way of preparing yourself, of cultivating a taste for it?

1. As familiarity is the first commandment of the music lover, you should use every opportunity to hear modern sacred music. You cannot like something you know nothing about.

This can be done in at least four ways, all of them offering at least the possibility of hearing this type of music: (a) by attending choral concerts, particularly those of the church college choirs, (b) by listening to such church choirs as occasionally sing modern music, (c) by participating in church music clinics and choral schools, and (d) by listening to recorded performances of modern choral works.

Apart from these opportunities, there is serious secular music in the modern idiom. Give yourself the benefit of hearing it with a view to understanding it, of being spoken to by it.

2. It is helpful to remember that, as one must cultivate a taste for certain foods, most people must develop a taste for, or learn to "hear," modern music. Generally, appreciation doesn't arrive in full bloom. Almost all of us can recall certain pieces which didn't appeal to us at first, but which, on successive hearings, unfolded their beauties until we saw them for the masterpieces they are.

3. Insofar as possible, listen with an open mind to the modern anthem your choir might be able to do. Get a sense of the piece as a whole, and then give it a chance to speak to you. You are under no obligation either to like or to dislike, but only to give the music a "50-50 break." No judge worthy of his position would try a case with his ears plugged, or make his decision before hearing it or before having carefully considered all the evidence.

Nor are you under any obligation to assume all modern music, even by composers of repute, is good—or bad. Some of it simply misses the mark as a vacuous display of technique; and some of it—more than you imagined—will open up vistas of beauty you never dreamt existed.

4. Study the music! This, of course, is part of the commandment of familiarity, but important enough to be listed separately. Get inside the music—and it will get inside you.

Modern music for your choir will require more study, for the simple reason that you are less familiar with it. Its demand that you give it study is both reasonable and fair.

Mark the difficult intervals, the complex rhythms, beat the varied patterns, decide how your choir can best manage this intense harmony or that, from whom the altos are to get their pitch for this attack, etc., etc. Frequently, to have anticipated a difficulty is to have solved it.

It is not difficult to get the music. Publishers will supply copies on approval, but this they cannot do unless you ask them to, stating in general the type of music you would like to see, the ability of your choir, and the not unimportant fact of the ability of your accompanist. It would perhaps be wise to stipulate that you are interested particularly in modern music—music, that is, which is progressive in its idiom.

5. Before you ask your choir to sing a "new song," you yourself must be convinced of its value. Short of the conviction which generates enthusiasm, you can scarcely hope to "sell" the piece to your choir. On the other hand, it has been demonstrated time and again that a choir can and will sing any anthem that has captured the enthusiasm of the director.

6. The taste for "modern" need not be—indeed, should not be—confined exclusively to music. In a sense, the Arts are one, as is shown in the cogent observation: "Modern art is *a way of thinking.*" The new idiom is not the property of music alone. Although the *means* for communication may differ, it flowers in all: poetry, painting, sculpture, drama, architecture.

Therefore, a part of your approach to a modern anthem

should include the broader preparation of understanding, of responding to the new in *all* the Arts. While one may not cover the whole range, any thoughtful effort in this direction will enhance your grasp of this "way of thinking," and, in so doing, equip you better to deal with your anthem.

The New Song and the Choir

Given the opportunity to become intimately acquainted with a modern anthem, it should be expected that the choir's response will be favorable. That it may not be to begin with should neither surprise nor discourage you. It should be remembered that the choir, too, is entitled to its period of orientation, learning, and adjustment.

You have several definite advantages as you put a modern anthem into rehearsal:

1. Radio and TV have exposed your choir members to a vast amount of music in the modern idiom. Thus, the ability to "hear" is not at zero; it is not a totally foreign language.

2. Music programs in the public schools—a continuing challenge to church musicians—include a good deal of modern music. Many students are ripe for modern music in their church choirs; they "hear" its harmonies, they like its rhythms, they enjoy the challenge.

3. The number of college graduates in parish choirs increases year by year. These people, many with wide musical experience, will tend to favor the "new song."

It is a serious mistake to underestimate the tastes and ability of your choir. But at the same time, you probably had better not assume that the desire for modern music already exists in 100% of your membership, or that the ability to perform it is immediately present.

If the modern idiom is foreign to the singing experience of your choir, your choice of the first such number you give them should be judicious. The problems, both of harmony and rhythm, should be minimal: enough to challenge, but not so much as to discourage; enough to whet the curiosity of the choir, but not so much as to destroy interest.

Since, as was shown in an earlier discussion, the melodies (often in every section of the choir) are actually quite lyric—though surrounded by dissonant harmony, the parts should be rehearsed individually for their melodic value. This will alleviate fears of "no singing melody," "a tuneless string of notes," etc. Then, when every section can sing its song confidently and expressively, put the parts together. Keep the melodies singing; the harmony will take care of itself.

Despite fairly extensive exposure to modern music outside the Church, the choir probably has heard little, if any, inside. Because your choir is accustomed to the stereotype, its chief problem *will be that of "hearing" the new idiom* and then expressing religious sentiments through these new tonal relationships and rhythmic patterns.

The New Song and the Congregation

While it is not always true, it is likely that the more musical members of the congregation belong to the choir. Therefore, if the choir needs time for orientation and adjustment—if it has to learn to "hear" in the new idiom— the congregation must be given even more consideration

Not only are its average musical ability and receptivity lower than those of the choir, but it is at a disadvantage in not having become acquainted with the anthem through intensive rehearsing. On Sunday morning, then, the congregation "hears it cold," and the experience can be mildly shocking, to say the least.

Antipathy toward the new and fondness for the old is as true of a congregation as of men generally; but it is possible that the congregation may feel somewhat more deeply about a modern anthem. Through years of association with more conventional church music, certain styles have come to be regarded as "right and holy." (They may very well be, but the notion that they are *exclusive* cannot be sustained—any more than one could support the old man who was both angry and disillusioned when he discovered that the Bible was not originally written in Norwegian).

This attitude on the part of the congregation, however wrong, cannot be summarily brushed aside. It must be reckoned with—sympathetically.

You should, therefore, recognize the existence of prejudices, and not be too surprised if the response to the new is less enthusiastic than the fondness for the old and the familiar. To this awareness you should bring your zeal as a director-educator, one who teaches and leads the way. The congregation, after all, expects you to do this—to the best of your ability.

The educational process begins with the simple, as it did in the choir. Problems of listening should be few, but enough to arouse interest and, perhaps, to make a few worshippers think, "This music gave new meaning to the text." It is helpful to print the text in the bulletin so that the congregation has before it the matter whose spirit and meanings the music intensifies.

The process may take the form of song services and concerts at which you discuss the "new song" and the choir demonstrates by singing. The congregation participates by singing the familiar setting of a beloved hymn, and then is asked to note how a contemporary composer has used modern techniques to convey the spirit of the same hymn. Or the congregation may actually sing a hymntune in the modern idiom (*God Be Merciful*, by Daniel Moe, is a fine example), and then listen as the choir sings the sturdy anthem the composer has built upon it. The choir may sing a group of anthems—or an entire concert — entitled "Modern Settings of Classic Religious Texts." The methods for interesting, effective, and inspirational teaching are many.

The role of your organist in such a program shouldn't be overlooked, for he can represent the "new song" with modern chorale preludes and progressive improvisations on well-known church melodies.

As the education does not begin with the complex, neither should you expect to complete it tomorrow. It is a gradual unfolding, a maturing process, an orderly growth.

It requires careful planning and selection, it needs time and effort, it must have understanding and vision.

The "new song" is worthy of every effort.

He hath put a new song in my mouth. Psalm 40:3.